EUGENE V. DEBS

D1129167

Praise for Eugene V. Debs: A Graphic Biography

"As socialists of Debs's era might say: 'here's the ammunition.' In addition to being a delightful biography of the railroad man from Terre Haute, this is a splendid genealogy of the struggles and ideas that energize today's socialist revival. Buy an extra copy and turn on a friend or workmate." —**Mike Davis**

"Eugene V. Debs implanted the searing notion of solidarity deep in the American soul, where it awaits rediscovery today. But we're going to need a few more men and women like Debs—selfless leaders capable of building movements across lines of race and gender. Fortunately, I see them springing up all around us." —**Barbara Ehrenreich**

"I see copies of this book furtively passed around the employee locker rooms of fast-food chains and mega-distribution centers throughout America where a new generation of wage slaves, with a taste for comics, will find inspiration in the story of Eugene V. Debs. The proceeds from the sale of this book thus go, indirectly, toward the abolition of capitalism." —**Ben Katchor**

"Eugene V. Debs: A Graphic Biography summons the spirit of our greatest American socialist, someone who inspired generations of reformers from A. Philip Randolph to Bernie Sanders." —**Bhaskar Sunkara**

"At a time when socialism has reentered the political vocabulary, it is wonderful to have this engaging book, introducing old-timers and a new generation to the greatest American socialist, Eugene V. Debs. A beloved labor leader, tireless battler against economic inequality, and defender of free speech, Debs's radicalism and commitment to social justice are more needed today than at any time since his death." —**Eric Foner**

"I must shamefacedly admit that, lefty though I am, I have known very little about Eugene Debs aside from the fact that he ran for president on the Socialist Party ticket three times, once while in prison, and that he was a pacifist. Now, thanks to Noah Van Sciver, Paul Buhle, Steve Max, and Dave Nance, I can proudly hold a conversation with the most knowledgeable Socialist historian. If one picture is worth a thousand words, this excellent combination of words and pictures is worth its weight in rubies." —**Trina Robbins**

"If Eugene Victor Debs could have chosen a twenty-first-century biographer, I am reasonably certain that he would have gone with Paul Buhle, the great custodian of socialist lore and champion of Debsian fellowship. This perfect retelling of the story of the great organizer and candidate captures more than the details of a radical life, it expresses the revolutionary spirit that made Debs the beloved comrade not just for his time but for ours." —**John Nichols**

"A century before Bernie Sanders and Alexandria Ocasio-Cortez, the American voice and standard-bearer for democratic socialist ideas was Eugene Victor Debs. Disturbingly, the battle lines of 1919 are again the battle lines of 2019: stemming the concentration of wealth in fewer and fewer hands, assuring women equal rights, securing the rights of workers to bargain collectively, opening our gates to immigrants. This is a biography for our time." —**Samuel Norich, President of the Forward**

EUGENE V. DEBS

A GRAPHIC BIOGRAPHY

ART BY NOAH VAN SCIVER
SCRIPT BY PAUL BUHLE AND
STEVE MAX, WITH DAVE NANCE

This book was made possible by the generous support of the Democratic Socialists of America Fund. The DSA Fund is a 502(c)(3) fund devoted to education and outreach about Democratic Socialism.

The Democratic Socialists of America Fund endeavors to demonstrate how an awareness of social democratic and democratic socialist values and policies would strengthen the quality of policy debates in the United States. The Fund also works to introduce young activists to the history and traditions of democratic socialism.

First published by Verso 2019
Art © Noah Van Sciver 2019
Script © Paul Buhle and Steve Max, with Dave Nance 2019

All rights reserved

The moral rights of the artist and authors have been asserted

1 3 5 7 9 10 8 6 4 2

Verso
UK: 6 Meard Street, London W1F 0EG
US: 20 Jay Street, Suite 1010, Brooklyn, NY 11201

versobooks.com

Verso is the imprint of New Left Books

ISBN-13: 978-1-78663-687-4
ISBN-13: 978-1-78663-686-7 (US EBK)
ISBN-13: 978-1-78663-685-0 (UK EBK)

British Library Cataloguing in Publication Data
A catalogue record for this book is available from the British Library

Library of Congress Cataloging-in-Publication Data
Names: Van Sciver, Noah, artist. | Buhle, Paul, 1944– author. | Max, Steve, author.
Title: Eugene V. Debs : a graphic biography / art by Noah Van Sciver ; script
  by Paul Buhle and Steve Max, with Dave Nance.
Description: Brooklyn, NY : Verso, 2019.
Identifiers: LCCN 2018033722| ISBN 9781786636874 (paperback) | ISBN
  9781786636850 (uk ebook)
Subjects: LCSH: Debs, Eugene V. (Eugene Victor), 1855-1926—Comic books,
  strips, etc. | Socialists—United States—Biography—Comic books, strips,
  etc. | Working class—United States—Biography—Comic books, strips, etc.
  | Graphic novels. | BISAC: BIOGRAPHY & AUTOBIOGRAPHY / Political. |
  BIOGRAPHY & AUTOBIOGRAPHY / Historical. | POLITICAL SCIENCE / Political
  Ideologies / Communism & Socialism.
Classification: LCC HX84.D3 V36 2019 | DDC 335/.3092 [B] —dc23
LC record available at https://lccn.loc.gov/2018033722

Typeset in Granjon by Sean Ford
Printed and bound by CPI Group (UK) Ltd, Croydon, CR0 4YY

TABLE OF CONTENTS

TIME LINE OF DEBS'S LIFE

1855   Eugene Victor Debs is born in Terre Haute, Indiana.

1875   Debs joins the Brotherhood of Locomotive Firemen.

1880   Debs is named editor of *Locomotive Firemen's Magazine* and grand secretary of the Brotherhood of Locomotive Firemen.

1884   Debs is elected to a single term as a Democratic state representative in the Indiana General Assembly.

1885   Debs marries Katherine Metzel.

1893   The American Railway Union (ARU) is founded and becomes one of the first unions in the United States to organize unskilled workers. Debs is elected president. The following year, it leads a successful strike on the Great Northern Railway.

1894   ARU members lead the Pullman Strike, which is broken by federal troops. Debs is sent to prison in Illinois, where he becomes a socialist.

1895   Debs leads the new Social Democracy movement to organize around his new socialist ideals and runs for president in 1900 on the Social Democratic Party of America ticket.

1901   Debs's Social Democratic Party and the Socialist Labor Party
merge to form the Socialist Party of America.

1904   Debs runs for president on the Socialist Party ticket.

1908   Debs's third run for president.

1905   The Industrial Workers of the World is formed by Debs, miners'
leader Big Bill Haywood, and other socialist and labor activists
to organize unskilled workers across entire industries.

1912   Debs wins more than 901,000 votes in his presidential run
(6 percent of the total) and leads a rising Socialist Party at its
apex of 118,000 members.

1917   An emergency national convention of the Socialist Party in Saint
Louis declares opposition to World War I and resists US entry
to the war.

1918   Debs delivers a speech against the war in Canton, Ohio, violating the wartime Sedition and Espionage Acts, which made it a federal crime to speak against the war and the military draft.

1919   Debs is sent to prison after an unsuccessful legal appeal.

1920   Debs runs for president for the fifth time and wins nearly a million votes for the Socialist Party from behind bars.

1921   Debs exits Atlanta Penitentiary and returns home to Terre Haute in a state of declining health.

1926   Debs dies at Lindlahr Sanitarium in Elmhurst, Illinois. Norman Thomas conducts his funeral from the front porch of the Debs home in Terre Haute.

1966   The Debs home is named a National Historic Landmark (now maintained by the Eugene V. Debs Foundation).

MORNIN' 'GENE !
When a chap has lost his grip,
An' Fate has 'im on the hip,
Er he's trekked the trails o' sin
Till his feet are tangled in
Tribbelation's toughest webs,
What he needs is Eugene Debs
To reorganize 'im, fer
'Gene's the champyin comferter.
At sich times, ef he should meet
Debs a-comin' down the street,
Then the clouds o' trouble roll
Frum his over-shaddered soul,
An' the skies are all serene
As he murmurs, "Mornin', 'Gene!"

—Walter Hurt

INTRODUCTION

The life of Eugene Victor Debs (1855-1926) has returned to public interest and sympathy in ways that no one would have expected five or ten years ago. "Socialism," contrary to liberal and conservative pronouncements, has made a comeback. The political campaign of Bernie Sanders during 2015-16, appealing to millions of young people but not them only, shocked the mainstream, Democrats as well as Republicans. The Wall Street crash of 2008, and the mass movements of Occupy and Black Lives Matter, almost seemed to have called a movement and a charismatic leader into being. To speak only of this comic's co-sponsor, Democratic Socialists of America has at this writing grown its membership to over 50,000 members, a height not seen in any American left group since the 1940s.

From another angle, Debs offers an American legend as big and meaningful as that of Johnny Appleseed (aka John Chapman) or Martin Luther King, Jr., two real life figures different in so many ways, but both of them firm believers in non-violence and the hopes for a finer outcome to the national saga. They were both martyrs, John Chapman isolated and destitute (if by choice) in an 1840s America full of raging violence and visions of reform, King felled by a racist assassin amid the radicalized 1960s. If we were to look at Debs in this way, the physically broken idealist who placed himself in the way of government persecution, and never recovered his strength after—then he, too, was a martyr.

But we may be sure that through his many labor struggles,

Debs himself would never have chosen "martyrdom" as his signature achievement or intent. Instead, "Solidarity," what he sometimes called "the Christ-like practice of Solidarity," signified an overcoming of brutal individualism, a self-confidence in human capacity that prompted him to say he would not lead workers into the Promised Land because someone else, some other foremost figure, could lead them out again. Debs, willing to be a leader, willing to sacrifice his health to this purpose, looked beyond himself and his own lifetime.

That "solidarity" took the form of "socialism" is due to the time and place of Debs's life. But if the time for "socialism," in a distinctly democratic form, has indeed come again, then we can better appreciate why a movement for the abolition of capitalism seemed an obvious step from the 1890s to the end of Debs's life. The aging Civil War veterans calling themselves "Abe's Boys" were among his most eager supporters. Even the great Carl Sandburg, visiting Debs in a sanitarium following his release from prison, argued that John Brown was more criminal than hero. Likely channeling the Union troops' own anthem ("John Brown's body lies a mouldering in the grave, his truth is marching on"), Debs adamantly disagreed with his younger friend. The blood price that Lincoln declared paid for the sin of black slavery might be redeemed in the abolition of wage slavery, for the good of the entire society and especially for the downtrodden themselves.

Many times in Debs' life, on the lecture or campaign trails, the great socialist was surrounded by children eager to present him with bouquets of flowers. If this detail seems maudlin or out of fashion, then we have lost something important that we need to regain.

Debs is the sweetest strong man in the world . . . and his spirit is more beautiful, than anything that I have seen in any man of my time . . . His genius is for love—the ancient, real love, the miracle love, that utterly identifies itself with the emotions and the needs and wishes of others . . . And that is why Debs was convicted of a crime—he was convicted because he could not open his mouth without declaring his solidarity and inward identity with his comrades who are in prison.

—Max Eastman, "The Trial of Eugene Debs"

1

THE RISE OF EUGENE V. DEBS

The rise of an American socialist movement, and of the young railroad unionist Eugene V. Debs to heroic status, is at once a classic saga of rising class consciousness and a unique, emphatically unprecedented convergence. It wasn't that socialism and socialists had not existed in the United States before. It was that the jagged route of previous false starts leveled once he stepped onto it.

This story has usually been told by way of unhappy contrast to Europe. Across much the continent and in Britain, by 1900 socialism had become a mass political movement of labor. In Germany above all, an intermittently repressed socialist party threatened to become the central fact of national life, from factories to parliament. No such organic development took place, however, in America, the most rapidly industrializing society of the mid- to late-nineteenth-century world. The unique, rebellious radical impulses of abolitionism, women's rights, dress reform (largely a product of the Yankee lower middle class), and others offered fresh approaches to the very idea of social change. Before these grand idealistic movements faded in the post–Civil War years, their commitments often clashed with those of the small craft unions, whose leaders mostly sympathized with the largely anti-reform and deeply racist Democratic Party and who were dedicated to organizing only the most skilled workers.

The Communist Manifesto first appeared in English west of the Atlantic in *Woodhull and Claflin's Weekly,* the newspaper of two well-funded socialist sisters who also ardently supported gender equality and leaned toward spiritualism. Victoria Woodhull and her followers comprised a majority of the United States' little socialist movement by 1870, including nearly all its American-born members, but soon found themselves expelled. The dour German immigrants who held the socialist franchise—with the express permission of Karl Marx—considered them improper representatives of working-class ideals. It was not a promising beginning. Indeed, one might say that this expulsion cut off the young socialist movement from the rich tradition of American radicalism of the 1840s to 1860s.

However, a deep economic depression, dramatized by the Great Railroad Strike of 1877, sent socialists into public office in a half-dozen states. The success of the little socialist groupings eager for European-style developments proved to be short-lived. Electoral failure rapidly followed, with reform-minded Democrats successfully reaching out to socialist constituencies. Along with "ballot stuffing" and the suppression of socialist votes, this cooptation became a regular pattern for generations.

Almost nothing went as predicted for American socialists, although some unexpected developments stirred revolutionary imaginations. During the 1880s, Chicago—with its rebellious working class—was widely called "Little Paris," invoking the memory of the 1871 Paris Commune. Out west, striking miners and company militias met each other with carbines firing. A mighty union half a million strong emerged as if from nowhere in 1884, with the unsocialistic name of the Knights of Labor. In a few more years, a novel about a future socialist society—*Looking Backward,* by Massachusetts newspaperman Edward Bellamy—became one of the bestselling English-language books of the second half of the nineteenth century. By the millions, Americans seemed to be thinking about class and even about socialism.

Young Gene Debs, leader of the typically exclusionary Brotherhood of Locomotive Firemen, hardly knew what to make of such developments. Had he dabbled in the socialist politics of the day, he might have been still more confused. A second

American-born socialist contingent, those speaking English as a first language, joined the little Sozialistische Arbeiter Partei (Socialist Labor Party) in the later 1870s and then drifted away—a historic pattern of shifting membership within the American Left. Meanwhile, the few thousand steady socialist members until the early 1890s were overwhelmingly German-born, connected to the idea of socialism through the web of fraternal and gymnastic societies, local union assemblies, and a shared secular, urban immigrant culture. In New York, Chicago, St. Louis, Milwaukee, and a string of other cities, "Germania" emerged, a world unto itself. Its ambience, including family-style taverns with musical and dramatic entertainments, offered a respite from the fast-moving, violent, alienating American society.

Socialists had worse luck within organized labor. Leading craft-union figures, notably the former socialist Samuel Gompers, sought to win the labor movement away from socialistic sympathies once and for all—and by any means necessary, from threats and corruption to collaborating with employers and police against dissident unions. The labor leaders around Gompers were not necessarily so adamant. Some, especially those rising with the immigrant Jewish labor radicalism of the 1890s and after, were sympathetic to the socialists, if also eager to promote a working relationship with employers.

European socialists often wondered how the volatile class conflict in the young nation across the Atlantic had produced such conservative labor leadership. Opponents of socialism often pointed to the material wealth of US society and the relatively comfortable circumstances of the best-paid wage workers. These observers rarely noticed the contrast between the best paid and worst paid workers, notoriously among the most extreme in the world. Race, the legacy of slavery, and the presence of Asian workers in the late nineteenth century counted heavily, but so did the sheer variety of languages and cultures among recent immigrants. Employers used these differences to keep workers at each other's throats.

Gompers had observed the difficulty of crossing the lines of race and gender early on, and resolved to build a sturdy movement by locking the doors against the unfortunate. He testified in Congress against Chinese laborers, used racial slurs against African Americans, and showed little interest in organizing anyone outside the charmed circle of skilled workers, especially those of German and Irish extraction. Gompers represented a particular type of American labor leader, not so different from some of his successors. Naturally, he made himself the foremost foe of Eugene Debs.

Debs, for his part, might easily have risen near the top within this world of craft unionists, widely known as the "labor aristocrats." Increasingly, however, locomotive firemen fell under pressure from the vast railroad corporations. As the severe recession of the 1890s unfolded, Debs embraced the extraordinary pain and suffering of the poor, as well as the keen sense of disappointment widely felt from farm to city.

Why did Debs place himself in the path of organizational and personal martyrdom in 1894? Everyone reading this book may ponder the same question. Debs may have known that the success of his newly founded American Railway Union (ARU), which included workers of every skill level and pay, would demand more labor solidarity and less government repression than the odds allowed.

The call for ARU members and other railway workers to walk off the job in solidarity with the workers manufacturing luxury Pullman train cars in Illinois required extraordinary self-sacrifice by many thousands of or-

Rise like lions after slumber
In unvanquishable number
Shake your chains to earth like dew
which in sleep had fallen on you —
Ye are many — they are few.

—"masque of Anarchy" Percy Shelley

dinary Americans for little immediate gain. And yet, west of the Mississippi, they did strike en masse. Had the craft unions offered them sufficient solidarity, and had the federal government not extended an unprecedented repression against a thoroughly nonviolent work stoppage, they might even have won. It was not to be.

Debs did something extraordinary in defeat: he led thousands, not all of them ARU members, toward the planned creation of a utopian, cooperative colony. Though it was a popular idea of the time, greatly enhanced by both massive unemployment and the popularity of Edward Bellamy's novel *Looking Backward,* it could not succeed. But by then

Debs had become a national figure.

The next and inevitable step awaited. A fragmented, overwhelmingly foreign-born socialist movement made up of socialist Germans, Jews, and others who had waited for years (the Germans for several decades) for the arrival of a "true American" with wide appeal, found their veritable savior in the railroad man. They belonged to Debs and Debs belonged to them: a complicated but vitally important connection for American socialism, for the labor movement, and for the wider idealist hopes that had remained alive since abolitionist days. Perhaps the nation could become more than a center for production, commerce, and consumption.

TERRE
HAUTE, INDIANA

NOVEMBER 5th, 1855...

On l'appellera Eugène, comme le grand humaniste Eugène Sue.*

Oui, et Victor en hommage à Victor Hugo!**

1835, Daniel Debs has been sent from the French district of Alsace by his merchant father to study in Paris, where he becomes devoted to literature, refusing to join his father's business.

Eugene Debs's mother, Marguerite, was a worker in one of his father's factories. Daniel married her over his father's objections.

*We'll call him Eugene for the great humanistic novelist Eugene Sue.
** Yes, and Victor after Victor Hugo!

Only a decade before Debs's birth in Terre Haute, another great American dreamer died in Indiana, a railroad ride away. The legendary but also very real John Chapman, "Johnny Appleseed," breathed his last in Ft. Wayne, in 1845. Did Gene, in his boyhood, learn about John Chapman? Not every child in America heard about Johnny, apostle of non-violence and peace. But perhaps Gene did.

Je vois que tu as un de mes poètes préférés, Percy Shelley, cet anglais qui a soutenu la révolution française.*

* I see you have found one of my favorite poets: Percy Shelley, the Englishman who supported the great French Revolution.

Rise like lions after slumber
In unvanquishable number
Shake your chains to earth like dew
Which in sleep had fallen on you—
Ye are many—
they are few.

—"Masque of Anarchy" Percy Shelley

Desperation Strikes!

In 1877, as railroad corporations lower wages further and fired workers outright, communities from New York to Missouri struck back with train stoppages and rioting. For a week, socialists, many of them German immigrants, actually took over the cities of East St. Louis and St. Louis.

Union troops withdrawn from the South crushed what had become a "general strike" of all St. Louis's workers. Afterwards, around the country, the railroads returned to normal, but popular bitterness at the rich and powerful remained.

Debs, a Free Thinker?

As a founder of the city's new debating society, the Occidental Literary Club, I greet you and now I will recite Patrick Henry's famous oratory, "Give me Liberty or Give me Death!"

A woman's place is in the home not the voting booth, old Susan!

Ridiculous swine! Where's your husband?

Young Gene Debs personally rented a hall for Susan B. Anthony, woman suffrage leader, to speak in Terre Haute.

Young Debs was still too nervous to give a good speech. But he chose worthy subjects. He later said that "slavery never inspired one immortal thought or utterance."

Gene, we have no angry Gods to fear — no hell to dread. Our duty is to reason fearlessly and to be kind to all during our own lifetimes.

Robert G. Ingersoll, Great Free Thinker of America.

EUGENE V. DEBS FOR STATE LEGISLAT...

The capitalist class, like a devilfish, has grasped workers with its tentacles and was dragging them down to fathomless depths of degradations.
Railroad strike after strike was being lost during the late 1880s and early 1890s, locomotive craft unions failed to support each other, and Debs pondered what to do.
...Perhaps unifying craft workers is not good enough. What can workers do when they unite?

In 1894, the Pullman Palace Car Company, producing the grand railway cars for the rich to travel in comfort, demanded wage reductions from the workers who lived and worked in the one-industry company town, just outside of Chicago.

• PULLMAN BANK •

PULLMAN GROCERY

* PULLMAN DRY GOODS *

Across most of the country west of the Mississippi River, railroad workers bravely took their stand, and railroad lines shut down for a week.

WE MUST WIN THIS STRIKE or accept the permanent control of our America by the corporations and their lackeys!

We are not on strike for ourselves. We are offering our solidarity for the oppressed workers in Pullman, Illinois and their families!

KING DEBS.

The populist insurgency in the West and South threatened to sweep away the two party system. But votes were stolen and populist supporters, especially African American voters, suppressed violently in the South. Nothing remained for reformers but to join the populist wing of the Democrats.

You shall not press down upon the brow of labor this crown of thorns; You shall not crucify mankind upon a cross of gold!

Senator William Jennings Bryan captured the Democratic party convention with his powerful rhetoric against the 'Gold Standard' in currency. Bryan's electoral defeat by William McKinley, in 1896, marked the end of political populism.

A cooperative rural colony out west...

Hmm... No... we cannot escape capitalism that way...

2

"DEBSIAN SOCIALISM"

"Debsian socialism" remains in the American lexicon as a vestige of the golden age of socialist popularity, and for good reasons. Debs's near-million-vote total in the presidential election of 1912 would have rendered the Socialist Party the "third party" in American politics, if the Progressive "Bull Moose" Party, which split from the Republicans under the leadership of Theodore Roosevelt, had not offered overpowering competition. For a few years before and after, socialists held hundreds of offices in many states outside the South (and some even there), along with a few elected representatives to Congress. The socialist cause seemed to be growing ever more powerful—until the United States entered the First World War in 1917. Everything about this success story, however limited in time, is connected with Eugene V. Debs.

How did historical developments pave the way for socialist influences? The nation grew more prosperous, fast becoming a global economic leader, but only through "boom-and-bust" cycles, leaving millions in abject poverty during downturns. Industry advanced, but accelerating mechanization replaced the well-paying skilled jobs established only a generation or two earlier. New floods of immigrants, overwhelmingly from Eastern and Southern Europe, offered employers low-wage opportunities to get rid of costlier and sometimes more resistant workers. Smaller farmers in the West and South, especially, suffered from advances in large-scale agricultural

production and distribution that left them behind or, worse, trapped them in tenant-farmer status. Meanwhile, the intimacy of small-town and rural life seemed to grow more distant as fewer people depended upon home-grown crops and household skills. Nostalgia flourished in the young nation—and turned bitter.

Against and alongside these trends, the rise of reform movements offered wide hopes for a better society to emerge. Since the late nineteenth century, socialist political parties had arisen one after another across Western Europe and far beyond. By 1900 or so, the Social Democrats were the largest party in Germany, the historic home of Karl Marx and younger-generation figures like Rosa Luxemburg. Socialist ideas circulated so widely that many

distinguished thinkers of the day, conservatives to radicals, concluded that a cooperative society would be the next stage in the development of world civilization. The sheer chaos of capitalism reinforced the impression that society at large was achieving economic growth at a terrible price. American socialists saw in front of them a daunting diversity of racial, ethnic, regional, and political loyalties.

A formidable, all-conquering American empire already threatened any progress toward a more democratic society. For generations, practically since the declaration of the Monroe Doctrine, US foreign-policy leaders had presumed the right to pressure governments throughout the Western Hemisphere. The US invasion of Cuba in 1898, along with its conquest of the Philippines in a brutal invasion that lasted a decade, marked a dramatic escalation. Nearly all socialists and many reformers and African American leaders felt compelled to oppose what came to be called imperialism.

Another problem came closer to home. The largest conglomeration of socialists, middle-aged and middle American, bore little superficial resemblance to the socialist proletarians of Europe. Foreign visitors and even New Yorkers could hardly understand that the *Appeal to Reason,* the nation's largest weekly political newspaper, came from small-town Kansas. A later study of the "Appeal Army," the volunteers who sought new subscribers, revealed a mostly middle-aged cadre, a combination of craft workers, small farmers, and ministers' wives—the very social types sometimes ridiculed by European Marxists. But they educated themselves, built local socialist chapters, and often published their own local newspapers.

They also got votes, up to a point. The presidential vote for Debs rose from 88,000 in 1900 to 400,000 in 1904, 420,000 in 1908, and 900,000 in 1912—proportionately strongest in Oklahoma until the approach of the world war. Debs's campaigns had special strength in more than a dozen German American districts, with Milwaukee in the lead, and became increasingly strong among Jewish voters in New York as the years passed. By 1912, more than seventy-five socialist mayors presided in twenty-three states, the largest number in the small industrial towns of Ohio, alongside three Christian socialist ministers. Even in the Deep South, socialist candidates ran strongly in Louisiana and Mississippi.

Meanwhile, newer European immigrants came to the Socialist Party. Before 1910, it was mainly Jews who seemed to be succeeding the Germans and Bohemians of the great upheavals of the 1870s and 1880s. The numbers of Slovenes, Croatians, Hungarians, Poles, Finns, and others grew steadily, often putting down local roots with clubhouses and fraternal societies in blue-collar neighborhoods. As we shall see in later chapters, the Industrial Workers of the World (IWW), founded in 1905 by Debs and other socialists and radical unionists, would successfully reach out to the populations at the bottom of the workforce—new immigrants, agricultural workers, and in some places, African American laborers.

By 1910, the movement for women's suffrage, which Debs had supported since his days in Terre Haute, appeared to be within striking distance of success. Debs's support for women's issues played well with suffragists, but also mirrored the complexities of his personality and experiences. He had defended prostitutes in Terre Haute against police abuse and public scorn. His sympathies extended to the urgent need for access to birth control. This indifference to "respectability" extended to his embrace of African American dignity and suffering, as against the respectable racism that permeated American society. Much of white Indiana viewed the legacy of the abolitionist martyr John Brown as one of mere terrorism. Debs, though, throughout his life, considered Brown one of the bravest and most important Americans. However, he regarded any special appeals to the African American worker as harmful to proletarian unity, a view abandoned by later socialists and Communists.

Even these remarkable facets of his personality do not begin to exhaust the sources of Debs's appeal. There had never, in the history of American socialists thus far, been any leader who so eagerly encouraged popular art, such as newspaper humorists and comic artists (some of the best of the day leaned toward socialism). Writers and artists critical of capitalism warmly returned his affection.

Foreign-born workers and their families who were drawn to socialist ideas (or brought such ideas over from the Old World) also seemed to adore, even worship, Debs, even more than the native-born. They feared prejudice along with class oppression, and Debs offered them hope and direction. A ninety-seven-year-old Slovenian woman and former hat makers' union leader, interviewed in 1981, recalled with excitement, "Gene Debs held my baby!" She held that memory dear.

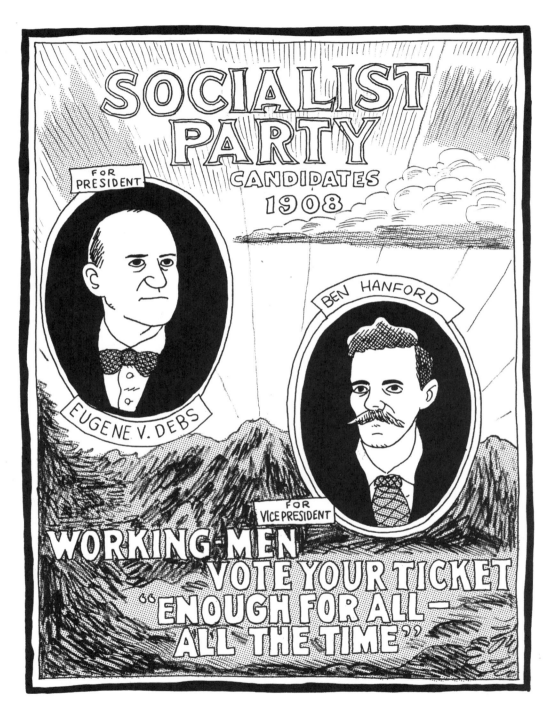

SOCIALIST EDUCATION!

Study circles gathered in small towns all the way to California to learn about Socialism. Civil War veterans, schoolteachers, ministers' wives, blacklisted railroad workers, they were respectable Americans, admired by their neighbors.

I am proud to be asked by Gene to help found the Intercollegiate Socialist Society, the first young people's socialist organization in the United States.

The romantic author of the best-selling *Call of the Wild*, Jack London was a close friend of Debs and a major celebrity.

At least two hundred thousand Filipinos were slaughtered in the one-sided American war for conquest. Debs wrote in 1897, as it began:

"There are thousands who are not swept from their feet by the war craze. We are opposed to war, but if it ever becomes necessary for us to enlist, it will be to wipe out Capitalism, the common enemy of the oppressed and downtrodden of all nations."

I suggest a new flag, with white stripes painted black and the stars replaced by the skull and crossbones.

MARK TWAIN SOCIALIST

EDUCATION
RELIGION
STEEL RAILS
BRIDGES

PHILIPPINES

CHINA

Redrawn from Emil Flohri, Judge, ca. 1900

Debs and the Poets
Camden, New Jersey...

Followers of Walt Whitman, including Whitman's friend Horace Traubel, founder of the Whitman Fellowship, looked to Debs as successor to the vision of the Great, Gray Poet.

Horace Traubel

WALT WHITMAN

To Eugene Debs by Sara Bard Field

Well, once in Cleveland, when I heard you speak

I sat upon the platform with my little son

Upon my lap and when your speech was done

You turned and laid your big hand on his cheek

And said, "My friend, such lads as this

Must finish what we old folks have begun—"

The crowd was surging round you but a kiss

You reverently gave him—Debs, that little lad

Cherished till death the words that you had said

And loved to think your hand had touched his head.

This is the anniversary of John Brown's execution, December 2, 1859. John Brown was the spirit incarnate of the Revolution, and his execution changed the destiny of the universe. The hated agitator is now the sainted savior, and his name ranks highest among the immortals.

Black and white socialists read the *Christian Socialist*, met together and prayed together.

White racists are ignorant, lazy, unclean, totally void of ambition, themselves and foul products of the capitalist system.

Debs had always wanted a child, but he and his wife could not. In 1910, they adopted the son of Kate's stepdaughter, after the stepdaughter suddenly died.

Our new son is a proud socialist. When he grows up, he will respect the rights of women.

Kate M. Debs

VOTES FOR WOMEN AND SOCIALISM FOR THE USA

Across the country, Socialist women organized separately as well as together with men, creating a women's National Committee. Their magazine, The Progressive Woman, was widely read.

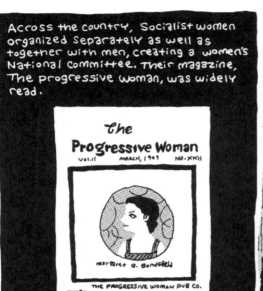

I was asked to write a column on Birth Control in the New York Call. We knew we were risking legal prosecution.

Margaret Sanger

...this is an informal birth control clinic, and it's illegal--

but we can provide you some devices that will help.

Dr. Antoinette Konikow, Socialist

Women deserve a right to control their own bodies! I salute the new birth control movement and condemn the government that wants to persecute them for it!

1912: The Greatest Socialist Campaign!

Debs at the height of his national popularity, was an unhealthy 57, with arthritis and other ailments, but the Red Special train made hundreds of stops across the country.

SOCIALIST PRESIDENTIAL SPECIAL

Through all the ages of the past the few have ruled and the many have served; the few have worn the purple of luxury and the many have struggled in poverty. The Socialist party is the political expression of the socialist movement in the emancipation of the working class from wage slavery.

3

TRIUMPH—AND THE EDGE OF TRAGEDY

In the saga of the Socialist Party, the years between 1912 and 1917 rushed by, each one containing enough events, both hopeful and tragic, for a decade. At the onset of this period, the socialists appeared to capture the very spirit of the emerging, dynamic working-class movement within a badly corrupt and class-divided society. At the close, they faced an orchestrated repression practically unknown in US history.

The striking images of workers' power in the Russian Revolution (recalled in John Reed's *Ten Days That Shook the World* (1919) and reaffirmed, but also subtly altered, in the 1981 film *Reds*) reflect real responses at the time. World revolution seemed, to many, on the agenda. It could happen! The excitement of the class conflicts in far-flung regions, however, somehow made less impression upon the American middle class than cultural conflicts around Greenwich Village, as "modernism" transformed the behavior, and especially the sexual habits, of the young. American culture was dragged out of the nineteenth century, seemingly all at once, by the advent of birth control, feminism, the campaign for women's suffrage, and the growing prestige of avant-garde art depicting the drama of the city and the lives of the poor. A little-understood reality of this era was the outward spread of bohemianism and the loosening of the previous generation's moral strictures, behavior formerly frowned upon within polite society. Free-spirited young working-class women were the real source of the ballyhooed, more middle-class "flappers" during the 1920s. Then there was the emergence of Harlem, flourishing after 1917 as the new global heart of Black political and cultural life.

The crowds that rushed to hear Debs and other socialist speakers in the 1910s included young working people loosened from the religious bonds of their parents and eager to find new ways of living. Young women might now become local union leaders or social reformers, sharing a hope for a cooperative society. Copies of *The Masses* magazine were likely read just as eagerly in Seattle as in Manhattan and Brooklyn by young people feeling the possibility of a new society. In this context, Debs—though part of the "old" labor radicals—became a modern, living saint, one whom Americans desperately needed.

These developments concealed a major demographic and political shift. The appeal of "progressive" and reformist but non-socialist candidates for local offices had diminished the socialist program among middle-class supporters by 1912. A genuinely progressive but non-socialist impulse, represented by Wisconsin governor Robert M. La Follette, contrasted with the bellicose (and racially tinged) nationalism of Theodore Roosevelt who defeated La Follette for the Progressive Party nomination that year. But in the public mind and in the press, Debs and La Follette were not so different: if monopolies could be controlled or broken up, the nation would advance. Undercut among the American-born, the Socialist Party meanwhile advanced rapidly among blue-collar immigrants.

The "new immigrants" and unskilled laborers Debs and the IWW had already embraced now made their mark upon wider social movements. The IWW faltered: partly from internal disagreements, mostly from the rival American Federation of Labor (AFL) and the pressure of employers against any organization of the low-caste worker. By 1914, the best days of the IWW were passing, and immigrant workers in particular were more likely to find their place within existing or newly launched AFL unions and the Socialist Party. The effect was complex and dramatic.

The Socialist Party of 1915 was not the Socialist Party of 1912, and the Socialist Party of 1917 was yet further from the "Debs Party" of the 1904 or 1908 campaigns. Debs became hugely popular among these new immigrants, as far as this can be ascertained. Education in socialist ideas was continuous, especially in the socialist clubhouses in growing immigrant neighborhoods of various ethnicities. But voting was often difficult for the foreign-born and was sometimes restricted by authorities. Labor action picked up the slack. With the outbreak of war in Europe, the labor market tightened and workers could more readily quit undesirable jobs. Both strikes and union organizing became easier, absorbing the energy of younger socialists in particular. In New York's garment centers, the socialist union leaders who had created power centers for themselves during the 1890s now proved bureaucratic and resistant to militant activity, opening the gates for more aggressive organizing and more radical politics—much of it led by young immigrant women.

The fear of war, and what it would surely bring, cast a dark shadow upon the horizon. Socialists had been writing about it since the US invasion of the Philippines, and Mark Twain campaigned against the horrors of imperial massacres large and small. Socialist magazines discussed, in essays by popular authors, the prospect of the end of civilization—more specifically, the end to the American experiment in democratic civilization, the consolidation of American empire, and the attendant state repression of dissent at home. Indeed, the war years did see mass arrests, and leftist publications were forced to close.

Americans continued to vote for socialists at the state and local levels in considerable number, including electing two socialists to Congress and many city officials. But the advancing momentum of the socialist vote, like Socialist Party membership, had mostly stopped. Antiwar writer Allan L. Benson polled less than 600,000 votes, a considerable number but a significant drop from Debs's 1912 total. Political repression would soon wipe out the socialist votes in Oklahoma, where the Socialist Party had gained the highest percentile in many counties. The future suddenly looked grim for those who believed socialism would be brought by the ballot.

The outbreak of World War I reshaped European socialist movements decisively, with uncertain echoes on American shores even before the United States' entry in 1917. Fixed beliefs and the older sense of confidence that education and voting would lead to

the triumph of socialism were now thrown into doubt, if not utter despair. In the veritable homeland of socialism, German leaders who only months earlier had sworn resistance to war caved in to the appeal of the government for armaments and the draft. English, French, and other socialist leaders, with honorable exceptions, also capitulated to the call for national defense—and in especially dishonorable cases, the call to expand imperial conquest of distant colonies. (The "revisionists" of German socialism, whose views had been famously explained by Eduard Bernstein, stood out in their insistence that empire was an economic lever for successful capitalism, presumably leading eventually to socialism.) Some Italian syndicalist leaders, including future fascist dictator Benito Mussolini, went over to support the war and

reap its potential fruits. American socialists experienced heightened nationalistic and other differences, within ethnic neighborhoods and beyond. The outlook was ominous.

The moment had arrived for a socialist-style pacifism. Norman Thomas, future leader of the Socialist Party, would quickly make a name for himself as a spokesman for humanitarian rationalism against the belligerent insanity that was to overwhelm so much of existing civilization for the rest of the century.

We can see from a distance that the US Socialist Party was neither automatically doomed nor exalted by the prospects of 1917, including the Russian Revolution. But the reality little resembled the path to socialism Debs had laid out in the *Appeal to Reason* a decade earlier.

There never was a magazine like THE MASSES, before or since.

The Masses
AUGUST 1915   10 CENTS

IN GEORGIA

The MASSES
JUNE 1913   10 CENTS

"Gee, Mag. Think of us bein' on a magazine cover!"

THE VILLAGE ART GAL

And there was never a bohemia like "The village" of those days.

SOCIALISM IS INTERNATIONAL!

WE WANT BREAD AND ROSES TOO!

Mill workers of more than a dozen nationalities went on strike in Lawrence, massachusetts, in early 1912. They were led by Elizabeth Gurley Flynn, "The Rebel Girl," and Italian-American labor poet Arturo Giovannitti. The strike was won but the leaders were jailed.

The arrest of Giovannitti and Joseph Ettor on charges of "conspiracy" stirred protest around the world, especially in Italy.

LAWRENCE, MASS.

THE LAWRENCE WAY

ART YOUNG

Socialist novelists described an America after the cataclysmic war had wiped out civilization.

Jack London's best-selling novel, The Iron Heel, described something closer to the triumph of Fascism.

VIVA ALLENDE

4

MARTYR DEBS

The sight of Eugene Debs on trial and in prison for speaking against the war, a dramatic example of the wartime repression of civil liberties, was the bitterest experience of a generation for many socialists. "Preparedness," the code word anticipating US entry into war, was used to justify whipping up antisocialist hatred through blatant government propaganda, spuriously patriotic marches and rallies, and the insistence that anyone opposed to American participation supported the "Huns," the hated Germans. Decades later, historians and socialists who lived through this period would speculate on the strangeness of the Woodrow Wilson administration's claims that world democracy depended on jailing IWW "Wobblies" (with long sentences) and silencing all who questioned the war. The Wilson administration also quietly supported orchestrated mob violence against immigrants and African Americans, creating a permanent repressive apparatus that was later renamed the Federal Bureau of Investigation. Generations of activists ever afterward would be persecuted, their movements infiltrated and their efforts disrupted, at moments of national stress.

The catastrophe that fell upon the Socialist Party also came, of course, from the further left. The socialist parties of Europe discredited themselves (and not only among socialists) by supporting the wars conducted by their countries' armies, historically viewed as the worst enemies of the socialist and labor movements. American socialists heroically, if not always consistently, opposed US entry and the war slaughter at large. The success of the Russian Revolution led to the formation of the Third International and the creation of new Communist parties around the globe, in the expectation that world revolution was soon to come. This prediction turned out to be worse than mistaken. But the damage had been done here at home: in 1919, two Communist parties emerged almost simultaneously, warring against each other and against the Socialist Party. Both drew their members from the ranks of socialists.

Wilson's postmaster general, Albert Burelson, denied Second Class mailing permits to the socialist press, an act that proved perhaps more devastating than the jailings, the beatings, and the loss of party members to the Communists. Hundreds of English-language socialist papers, most of them weeklies, depended upon mail service; being refused it shut them down as effectively as arresting the staff or smashing the print room. Meanwhile, the mainstream press tarred socialists as disloyal Americans and possible "German agents"—a dangerous slander given the high level of anti-German vigilante violence. Socialists lacked the means to fight back, although sympathetic lawyers acted heroically to assist them against overwhelming odds and mounting legal expenses.

Immigrants, the section of the Socialist Party naturally most drawn to news about events abroad, actually escaped this suppression to some extent. Finnish, Hungarian, Polish, Greek, Bulgarian, and other non-English socialist newspapers continued to circulate in urban neighborhoods where English speakers, including the authorities, were unlikely to be able to read them. Tragically, many community divisions over the war, reflecting the situation in the homeland, also disrupted and in some cases badly limited ongoing local socialist activities. For "homeland" reasons, Slovenes thus supported the war, while their erstwhile Croatian counterparts lined up against it. Italian radicals similarly divided sharply (Italy itself changed sides as soon as the war began), and Polish socialists were overwhelmed by nationalists, reflecting the ongoing civil war at home. The new Communist movements drew primarily upon groups with homelands in Russia or not far from its borders. This demographically transformed left finally recovered—but not on the pre-1919 scale of members, and the Socialist Party remained badly diminished to less than half its prewar size.

Eugene Debs, imprisoned, could only read or learn from visitors about the complexities facing the socialists and the labor movement that had once looked to him for leadership and inspiration. Strikes and unionization raced ahead, with some socialistic unions (especially the Amalgamated Clothing Workers of America, or ACWA) taking on thousands of new members even as the IWW was persecuted and driven into the margins. A national strike of steelworkers for unionization and the near-weeklong Seattle General Strike of 1919 further dramatized labor's energy and its hopes for a better future. AFL leaders, especially Samuel Gompers, embraced the growth of unions—except for independent unions, like the ACWA—but also embraced legal repression as the perfect right of a state at war. Riots against Black communities (Gompers, like the Justice Department, blamed African Americans for the "trouble") meanwhile underlined racists' determination to push back against an African American population that was rapidly moving north, seeking employment and a re-

spite from hardening racial segregation in the South. In some locations, especially Chicago, veteran socialists and sections of the union movement fought back, offering Black communities a public defense against the murderous 1919 "white riot." But this was not common enough to hold back a conservative shift. The Ku Klux Klan, emboldened by the success of the film *Birth of a Nation,* launched another national campaign of organized hatred and political pressure on the mainstream.

This was no longer an America that Debs could easily understand. Hundreds of thousands of Americans, disillusioned with the war, were renewing their rebellious impulses, voting for their hero and voting local antiwar socialists back into office. But the Socialist Party no longer had the means to build upon these modest successes as a political machine. If the 1917 Bolshevik Revolution continued to appeal to the young, larger numbers turned their rebellion in different directions, from short skirts and freer love to European exile. Others turned to the more usual pleasures of private life amid the prosperity that the 1920s brought to wide sections of the American middle classes.

Early 1917

"President Wilson has cut diplomatic relations with Germany.

U.S. entry into war looks certain..."

WAR RAGES IN EUROPE

We socialists have always known that if war came, the government would repress anyone who resists.

Preparedness parade in New York City...

AMERICAN DEFENSE SOCIETY

AMERICAN PROTECTIVE LEAGUE

Worse is yet to come.

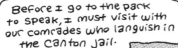

Before I go to the park to speak, I must visit with our comrades who languish in the Canton Jail.

remember the jailed draft protesters, and others persecuted for speaking their minds! I would rather a thousand times be a free soul in jail, like our comrade Rose Pastor Stokes, than to be a sycophant and coward in the street!

Nimisilla Park

CANTON WORKHOUSE

Ruthenberg | Wagenknecht | Baker

This war in a nutshell: The Master class has always declared the war; the subject class has always fought the battles! If war is right let it be declared by the people. You who have your lives to lose, you certainly above all others have the right to decide the momentous issue of WAR or PEACE!

I heard the whole thing - Debs urged disloyalty and resistance to conscription, violating the espionage act.

Tell me you'll indict and I will include it in my story!

Based on what you heard, I'm going to seek an indictment!

DEBS'S TRIAL BEGINS

CLAP CLAP CLAP CLAP CLAP CLAP CLAP

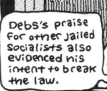

Order!! Order!! The bailiff will seize all those who were clapping, and bring them before the court! They are all to be cited for contempt!

Court adjourned!

CLACK CLACK CLACK

The court acknowledges that it was unduly vexed at your behavior yesterday. Still, decorum and respect for the tribunal must be maintained. Therefore, you are each required to pay a fine.

The prosecution's opening statement:

Gentlemen, in this trial we will prove Debs's words, and also his intent— which was to subvert the draft and interfere with the war effort— A goal set out in the St. Louis proclamation.

Debs's praise for other jailed socialists also evidenced his intent to break the law.

As did the fact that there were draft aged men there who might have been encouraged by him to ignore their duty.

Testimony begins:

Yes, I was there and I took a stenographic record of Mr. Debs's speech, at your request—

Then Mr. Steiner, tell us what Mr. Debs said next.

Uh— wait— I may have it—

I didn't get it all. There were a lot of words- uh let's see-- I'm sorry...

Don't feel too bad, your abilities were unfairly taxed!

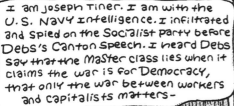

I am Joseph Tiner. I am with the U.S. Navy Intelligence. I infiltrated and spied on the Socialist Party before Debs's Canton speech. I heard Debs say that the Master class lies when it claims the war is for Democracy, that only the war between workers and capitalists matters—

The United States rests its case.

You rest? No, we rest!

I seek only the opportunity to speak directly to the jury.

And that the St. Louis proclamation should be followed.

I have been accused of having obstructed the war. I admit it, gentlemen I abhor war. I would oppose the war if I stood alone...

I admit being opposed to the present form of Government.

You may hasten the change, you may retard it; you can no more prevent it than you can prevent the coming of the sunrise on the morrow.

I admit being opposed to the present Social System. I am doing what little I can, and have been for many years, to bring about a change that shall do away with the rule of the great body of people by a relatively small class and establish in this country an industrial and social democracy...

...I believe in the right of free speech, in war as well as peace. I would not, under any circumstances, gag the lips of my bitterest enemy. I would under no circumstances suppress free speech!

MARTYR DEBS — 87

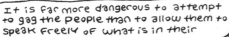

It is far more dangerous to attempt to gag the people than to allow them to speak freely of what is in their hearts...

What you may choose to do with me will be of small consequence after all. I am not on trial here.

There is an infinitely greater issue that is being tried today in this court, though you may not be conscious of it.

American institutions are on trial before a court of American citizens.

THE COURT IS ADJOURNED

AIR! AIR! Give her some air!

What happened?

Quickly! See that she's given aid!

She wanted to give you flowers, but she fainted, Mr. Debs!

Later:

Jury Foreman

Our verdict, your honor.

VERDICT

We the jury find the defendant guilty of having:

Count 1. Attempted to incite insubordination, disloyalty, mutiny and refusal of duty in the military and naval forces.

Count 2. Obstructed or attempted to obstruct the recruiting and enlistment service.

Count 3. Used language intended to incite, provoke and encourage resistance to the United States and to promote the cause of the enemy.

Schenk Decision!

Debs Decision!

Schenk Decision: If speech which is intended to result in a crime posed a "clear and present danger" of succeeding, it can be punished. Schenk v. U.S. 249 U.S. 47 (1919)

If the intent of the speech was to encourage those present to obstruct the recruiting service and such encouragement was directly given, the speech is not protected. 249 U.S. 211 (1919)

The reaction to the court's rejection of your appeal?

It's a ruling class court; it could not have been otherwise. Great issues are not decided by courts, but by the people. They will be heard from in due time.

April 13, 1919 Many railroad men were saddened that they had to work the train taking Gene Debs to jail that day.

I'm sorry, Kate - that was the news I had feared. I must report to the penitentiary in Moundsville immediately.

Dear Theo, Warden Terrell has been kind - a light job in the hospital, freedom to read, liberal visitation. The inmates are decent men all... This, as well as my sense of the presence of those who have gone before me, keeps me from despair...

Debs's prized possessions: A candle and a button which belonged to John Brown, a hero to Debs.

May 1, 1919 May Day demonstration, Cleveland, ohio...

"The Red Scare is a smoke screen, making protesters into "Anarchists" and "Bolsheviks..."

Arresting or even deporting them! And race riots are blamed on the Bolshevik Revolution!

Debs, I know you have been here 2 months, but I must inform you that you are being transferred to the U.S. Penitentiary in Atlanta, Georgia, effective immediately.

—why? What have I done?

WARDEN

I'm sorry about the hassle, I will ask the warden there to be lenient with you as I have, but you may find it harder there.

And so in Atlanta... I want no accommodations that my fellow prisoners go without. I would rather be in the block, held all day in a hot 6-man cell, wearing prisoner's stripes just as _they_ are!

Debs, the prisoners love you for your kindness and generosity.

But your empathy risks your health!

Have you any news regarding Eugene Debs? We heard he suffers from heart problems, terrible headaches, and kidney problems.

It won't be taken well if Debs dies under my supervision!

Debs, I will not have you die on me. You will now be assigned a light-work job in the hospital, and a private room there.

No one can begrudge him decent treatment. Debs is a hero...

Senator Harding, I'm Clyde Miller. I fought in France after Debs was sent to prison. I've changed my views since then. I know you're running for president in November and I urge you to consider the release of Debs if you win.

We shouldn't have been in that war... I know it. If I win this election, I'll look into freedom for Debs by July 4th of next year.

The Chicago Tribune

RUSSIAN BOLSHEVIKS NATIONALIZE WOMEN!

The Russian communists seem to be accused of everything except... splitting up our socialist party!

Morris Hillquit

SUPPORTERS OF A NEW, COMMUNIST MOVEMENT IN THE UNITED STATES SPLINTERED INTO FURIOUSLY HOSTILE FACTIONS, EACH INSISTING UPON BEING THE "TRUE" COMMUNISTS.

You're not true communists!

We are!

5

THE DEBS LEGACY
NORMAN THOMAS, MICHAEL HARRINGTON, BERNIE SANDERS

Eugene Debs's legacy for the twenty-first century is a struggle for survival and for dignity, leading away from capitalism and toward a cooperative society. Has progress been made, thanks to a push from the socialistic left? Yes, in many ways—no matter how much that progress is now under threat.

The pressures that socialists and others have placed upon government officials, especially elected Democrats, at the local, state, and national levels since the 1910s have enhanced living standards, made higher education more accessible, and introduced Social Security (among other entitlements) and rudimentary environmental protections. The right to organize a union remains law, even

under worsening conditions and restrictions. Socialists and their allies have successfully supported labor mobilizations and more complete civil rights for all. Gains that socialists, including Debs, were beaten, jailed, and sometimes murdered for are part of our common story.

Despite the backward slide since the 1980s, these are great accomplishments. Meanwhile, as Debs warned, empires (emphatically including the American empire) have not ceased warring against each other. The racism Debs attacked has not gone away, despite so much effort and so many hopes to the contrary. The military-industrial complex, known in Debs's time as "war profiteers" or "merchants of death," has expanded wildly and continues to threaten all social progress and, indeed, all life on the planet. Peace is a socialist struggle.

Socialists today, pressing for immediate reforms but also holding out the promise of abolishing capitalism, face tactical dilemmas that Debs would easily have recognized. They also face contradictions that have perplexed and maddened past socialist leaders. Perhaps the experiences of the last century within the left can serve us well, if we try to understand them sympathetically.

After Debs, the socialist movement in the United States could not help changing significantly. Before Debs —which is to say, before 1900— socialist parties had been small, highly unstable, and for the most part invisible to English-language readers and activists. The end of the Debs era meant, for almost a decade, a return to the shadows. For aging socialists of the 1920s—the shock troops of local work—too few consolations existed. For many young radicals, Russia held out an aura of global revolution, if definitely not an accurate view of what an American socialism might look like.

For the next twenty years and more, Norman Thomas would be the central figure within the Socialist Party. There were a few high points, especially during the 1932 presidential campaign, when hopes ran wild. Thomas's actual vote, about 885,000 that year, is impressive but seemed to eager socialists of the time a terrible disappointment. For millions of Americans, including many who did not actually vote for him, Thomas managed to become "Mr. Socialism." Like Debs before him, Thomas conveyed a spiritual quality: the faithful could become better people as well as helping to create a better society by embracing his message.

Norman Thomas and the organizational apparatus of the Socialist Party lacked the opportunity to return socialists to their central status within the left. The aura of electability and, beyond that, the certainty that, with enough socialist education, working people would lead the way to socialism—these hopes had been shattered amid war, repression, and bitter disappointment in the European socialist parties.

Perhaps the inclinations of the European-born, blue-collar socialists in many US cities and factories best show the underlying demographic shift on the left. Croatians,

Hungarians, Lithuanians, and other groups whose home parties and relatives stood close to the new Soviet Union felt an affinity to the global Communist movement. The alternative, as far as they could understand, was something increasingly like fascism and laced with anti-Semitism. Considerable numbers of Greeks, Ukrainians, Finns, and the newest, most impoverished Jewish immigrants likewise leaned toward the Communists. Communists also offered something special to African Americans: encouragement of certain trends in black nationalism. This policy was later reversed, but it made the "Negro question" the priority that it had never previously been in most of the American left.

The new American Communist movement, which began in extreme isolation, grew more successful in time. Communists soon had a vital press and blocs of activists in ethnic communities, unions, and legal-defense groups. Likewise, significant numbers of talented intellectuals and artists, Black and white alike, offered work in fresh magazines and newspapers, community choruses, theater, and other cultural venues. Communists also led great campaigns against injustice, such as the effort to spare famed anarchists Sacco and Vanzetti from execution by the state of Massachusetts on trumped-up charges of robbery and murder. Many other such campaigns followed.

Never mind that the Communist Party repeatedly flubbed political and labor opportunities, thanks mainly to changing orders from abroad. Never mind that Socialist Party membership, at the dawn of the 1930s, remained slightly higher than Communist membership, thanks mainly to reliable old-timers and the early failures of the Communists.

The rise of the unemployed movement at the height of the Depression, in the early 1930s, offered the Socialist Party one of its last major opportunities for membership and influence. The Unemployed Leagues organized at least as vigorously as the Communist-led Unemployment Councils and lacked the Communists' unrealistic expectations of imminent revolution. Soon, as the worst of the economic crisis died down, the two unemployed movements merged and the Communists exerted greater influence. By the mid-1930s, they grasped better than socialists did the growing imperative to work for re-

forms within newly expanding government agencies.

Moscow's 1935 declaration of a Popular Front Against Fascism had tossed "revolution" out the window, freeing American Communists and their allies to play a vital role at the leftward edge of the New Deal. Within the new industrial union movement—which was adamant about organizing all workers in a particular industry, not just the skilled ones—and the widening public-arts community, in civil rights and the struggle for a pluralistic society, Communist mobilizers and sympathetic "fellow travelers" offered inspiration and skills aplenty. The socialists were left behind.

The Socialist Party remained deeply democratic and consistent in its aims, even as the Communists careened from "line" to "line" as the political needs of the Soviet Union changed. Yet socialists could gain little traction. There were important exceptions. Idealistic young people drawn to the rhetoric and aura of Norman Thomas mirrored his sentiments for social justice and also for peace.

Young socialists in the Student League for Industrial Democracy rallied college students to march and educate their fellow students against the threat of war. Large demonstrations, walkouts, and "peace day" proclamations by shrewd university presidents (with classes suspended for a day) revived the socialist youth movement. By the later 1930s, as fascism threatened, this student peace movement faded.

Old-time socialist loyalists, ever fewer, bravely remained at their work. Holding onto membership and a voter base, especially in parts of heavily German American Wisconsin and Pennsylvania, socialists continued to elect local officials. They also retained many followers among the local and national leaders of the new industrial unions in the Congress of Industrial Organizations as well as the old AFL.

Loyal socialists continued to see themselves as the left-wing alternative to the hugely popular Franklin D. Roosevelt and the New Deal. But the moment had truly slipped away. Norman Thomas, gaining a bitterly disappointing 188,000 votes in 1936, ran poorly against Roosevelt, especially in New York State, where an American Labor Party ballot line allowed voters to support Roosevelt as well as their own union-led political movement. Votes for socialists—rather than Republicans or Democrats—turned into socialists' chief survival strategy, but also their greatest dilemma. They became a "protest" party, with ever fewer electoral victories beyond the local level.

Conflicts within the Socialist Party, as much the result as the cause of this isolation, further weakened the organization and made it still more dependent upon Norman Thomas's persona. Splits and divisions soon reached new heights . . . or depths. Followers of Leon Trotsky, few but strong in their criticism of Stalin and the failures of the US Communist movement, merged into the Socialist Party. Furiously contentious, they devoted considerable energies to attacking Communists and fellow socialists. Thomas himself directed their expulsion from the Socialist Party, but they had already demoralized significant parts of its remaining following, especially among the young.

Norman Thomas sometimes seemed like a one-man human rights campaign, even with a band of devoted supporters behind his efforts. He joined socialist H. L. Mitchell's Southern Tenant Farmers' Union campaign to bring white and black tenant farmers of the South into victory over the planters. Likewise, he personally challenged, at great personal risk, the abusive officials in Jersey City, New Jersey, defending free speech in the city's streets. Again and again he became a public hero, a living symbol of what a socialist could be and do.

One more grand push for a national peace movement in the late

1930s—this time against US entry into another world war—briefly gained Norman Thomas a wider following, if not many new members. Too soon, Thomas found himself uncomfortably allied with politically conservative isolationists. The war, as Thomas warned, would surely make militarism and militarization a sweeping, permanent, and destructive part of American life. But there was nothing to be done, with war in Europe impending.

The Socialist Party staggered onward, but mostly downward. Thomas's presidential vote sagged from 117,000 in 1940 to under 82,000 in 1944, then a bit upward to 143,000 in 1948—his last race and the party's last presidential race of significance. Thomas himself aged without ceas-

ing to be "Mr. Socialism," the grand moralist with steady radio and magazine appearances. He was widely seen as the public, liberal conscience of early Cold War America.

In a small movement of a few thousand mostly older-generation active members and a handful of outsized personalities, Michael Harrington emerged. A charismatic, popular author and lecturer and a favorite of New York banquets and college crowds alike, Harrington became the natural successor to Thomas. Tragically, for reasons personal as well as political, Harrington could not place himself at the head of the vast movement against the US war on Vietnam.

In part, this difficulty was both generational and cultural. Neither Harrington nor his trusted advisors could comprehend the new radicalism that effectively organized blue-collar populations, for instance in the "GI coffeehouse" movement, where institutions like the Oleo Strut in Texas met young men in basic training with invitations to talk, drink, or smoke marijuana together. The issue of universities' complicity in the war—from chemical research to develop napalm to spying on campus peace groups—did not seem to be within the political grasp of Harrington and his allies. Nor, for that matter, did women's liberation, viewed with great suspicion by some of Harrington's most trusted advisors, whose male-led world had nearly always seen women as lovers, wives, mothers, and helpers but not as political equals.

Harrington's mentor on labor issues, the veteran Trotskyist Max Shachtman, who decades earlier had been expelled from the socialist ranks, had meanwhile returned with a political following and an emerging strategy: socialists would influence the Democratic Party and the labor movement by supporting US foreign policy, including the war. Uncertain of his own views—whether the US should withdraw from Vietnam or await some negotiated solution—

Harrington suffered an emotional downturn. He dithered as the flagging socialist movement moved toward yet another set of sharpening internal divisions.

Harrington drew away from Shachtman's group, which emerged as the Social Democrats USA. Wildly hawkish, opposed to strict environmentalist regulations and affirmative action, Shachtman's following allied itself at the highest levels with the conservative leadership of the (now conjoined) AFL-CIO and its president, George Meany. Nor could Harrington bring himself to join another small faction retaining the official Socialist Party moniker, so as to run as a "third party" in local, state, and national elections.

Loyally supporting Democratic candidate George McGovern's presidential campaign of 1972, Michael Harrington and his followers founded a third and more promising socialist organization in 1973. The Democratic Socialist Organizing Committee (DSOC), a band of a few thousand socialists setting themselves against the daunting rightward drift of American politics at large, soldiered determinedly onward. A merger in 1981 with the New Ameri-

can Movement—an outgrowth of the vanished New Left—created a new identity for the leading group in the US socialist movement: the Democratic Socialists of America (DSA).

Through decades of economic recession, capitalistic recovery, a sharpening division of classes, and a substantial loss of progress on minority rights, DSA sought to pull the Democratic Party leftward. The election and re-election of California congressman Ron Dellums, a proud DSA co-chair, proved to be a rare triumph for an outright socialist at the federal level, even as constituencies within scattered cities moved politically leftward. Jesse Jackson's campaigns for the Democrats' presidential nomination, which many DSAers actively supported, were an-

other high point—followed by defeat and a characteristic feeling of disappointment.

Overall, Harrington's strategy presented a daunting task, made harder by a centrist and frequently hawkish drift among the rising bloc of powerful neoliberal Democrats and their corporate backers. His death in 1989 brought together in mourning liberal as well as socialist leaders, who understood what had been lost.

After the 1970s, DSAers and their allies continued to push for peace and equality. During 1995 and 1996, the overturn of the corrupted and conservative AFL-CIO leadership offered hope for a reinvigorated labor movement. Later, DSA members took part in the 1999

Seattle "Teamsters and Turtles" anti-globalization demonstrations, and then in 2011's Occupy movement. They naturally supported Black Lives Matter. Overcoming the early disadvantage of their failure to support the women's liberation movement, DSA marched into the future with fresh leadership, determined to support every aspect of gender equality.

The rise of Bernie Sanders, first as mayor of Burlington, Vermont, and then as US senator, marked a new course for popular socialist ideas. Sanders's campaign for the 2016 Democratic nomination created—or precipitated—a sudden, seemingly amazing interest in the DSA, specifically among so-called millennials. By 2018, its membership had reached the level of the Socialist Party during the early 1920s. Local DSA members took part in dozens, perhaps hundreds, of campaigns for progressive candidates. They could reasonably hope, this time around, to tilt the Democratic Party leftward, away from the largely regressive policies of its dominant factions on issues such as income redistribution and war.

The diminishment of the "neutral" space between Republicans and Democrats seemed to drive home this strategic option. Democratic socialism in the tradition of Debs continued to find new and old supporters and friends within electoral politics, public-sector unions, environmental organizations, and other groups seeking social and economic justice.

The idea of democratic socialism has been growing in popularity as the grim reality of capitalism, by vivid contrast, has grown ever more clear, especially among the young. This might be seen as the payoff—a new beginning—for the historic movements of American socialism. Perhaps the socialist ancestors, from every ethnic and racial group, are smiling down on today's socialists . . . and those of tomorrow.

NORMAN THOMAS FOR PRESIDENT

THOMAS

On some campus straw polls, the Socialist Norman Thomas wins. We are starting to call this Former minister "Mr. Socialism."

Can he get a million votes?

We were counted out and cheated, but we still got 850,000 votes!

NORMAN SOCIALIST

Americans want a Democrat to end the depression.

Yes, we are going to carry out a *New Deal* for the nation.

FDR

...Do you think the *New Deal* will carry out your Socialist program, Mr. Thomas?

The Socialist platform of 1932	Programs Adopted by the Roosevelt Administration
Legislation providing for the acquisition of land, buildings, and equipment necessary to put the unemployed to work producing food, fuel, and clothing, and for the erection of housing for their own use.	Various experimental communities were established towards these ends.
Old age pensions for men and women sixty years of age and over.	Provided by the Social Security Act, 1936, for those sixty-five years of age and over.
Health and maternity insurance.	Provided by the Social Security Act, 1936.
A federal appropriation of $5,000,000,000 for immediate relief for those in need to supplement state and local appropriations.	Federal Emergency Relief Act (Fera), May 12, 1933.
The six-hour day and the five-day work-week without a reduction in wages.	The Black bill for the establishment of a thirty-hour week was not passed by Congress.

I quipped at the time that FDR had carried out the Socialist platform — on a stretcher. Historians now say that many of the New Deal programs could be described as taken right out of my 1932 and 1936 platforms. We got some social gains.

But it was the Second World War that ended the depression.

Norman Thomas leads the struggle against militarization and war.

Student strikes, 1933-36, were mostly led by the Student League for Industrial Democracy, but faded as fears of Fascism grew.

I was proud to lead the "Keep America out of the war" Congress at the end of the 1930s. We knew that a war would threaten civil liberties, and produce a permanent military state.

But Nazism had to be defeated.

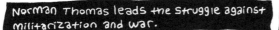

The New York Times

NOV·15 1938

LOW VOTE FOR NORMAN THOMAS' GUBERNATIONAL CAMPAIGN THROWS SOCIALIST PARTY OFF STATE BALLOT

1940 Norman was our presidential sacrifice. The American Left is larger than ever.

But with 116,000 votes and only a few thousand party members—

I don't see how much longer we can hold on.

Japanese Americans are treated like criminals. Their property, their houses, and businesses, will never be given back to them.

They deserve our support.

1950 After the Second World War, the Socialist Party faded further, Thomas ran for president once more, in 1948. Then he became just "Mr. Socialism," a voice for human rights.

THE DEBS LEGACY — 115

The Government has documented what this means to the bodies of the poor... But even more basic, this poverty twists and deforms the spirit. The American poor are pessimistic and defeated, and they are victimized by mental suffering to a degree unknown in suburbia...

The millions who are poor in the United States tend to become increasingly invisible. Here is a great mass of people, yet it takes an effort of the intellect and will even to see them.

I discovered this personally in a curious way. After I wrote my first article on poverty in America, I had all these statistics down on paper. I had proved to my satisfaction that there were around 50,000,000 poor in this country.

"The Other America"

Yet, I realized I did not believe my own figures. The poor existed in Government reports; they were percentages and numbers in long, close columns, but they were not part of my experience. I could prove that the other America existed, but I had never been there.

Your book is starting the revolution that we call our "War on Poverty," keep writing and come see us again.

Sargent Shriver

1963

This march is going to change America, Martin!

Still, we must be cautious. The president has warned us against saying anything radical.

Bayard Rustin

MLK

I have a dream...

The AFL-CIO will never endorse this march!

But the United Auto workers will!

George Meany

Walter Reuther

Here is a bulletin from CBS News: In Dallas, Texas, 3 shots were fired at president Kennedy's motorcade. The first reports say that president Kennedy has been seriously wounded...

What is this, another Orson Welles production?

Oh my goodness!

Quiet down!

CBS NEWS CBS NEWS CBS

When we got over the shock, we remembered that Lyndon Johnson, from a poor district in Texas, had the skills to get our anti-poverty program through congress.

U.S. stages the Gulf of Tonkin incident

The North Vietnamese have conducted deliberate attacks against U.S. Naval vessels in the Gulf of Tonkin.

The U.S. intends no rashness, and seeks no wider war.

LBJ

Formation of DSOC!

we are the Socialists who supported George McGovern and we're proud of it.

1973

MICHAEL HARRINGTON LEADS THE NEW DEMOCRATIC SOCIALISTS OF AMERICA

DAVENPORT, IOWA WELCOMES THE FOUNDING Convention of the new American Movement

In 1981, these two organizations will merge into the Democratic Socialists of America (DSA).

1976 Democratic party convention

EDWARD KENNEDY FOR PRESIDENT

1978

SOCIALISTS OUT-ORGANIZE CONSERVATIVE DEMOCRATS AT MID-TERM MEETINGS

Those Socialists, they keep winning the resolutions.

We could just abolish these mid-term party conventions.

Socialists and Labor

Today we announce our response to the Energy Crisis, we call it the "Citizen Labor Energy Coalition" or CLEC.

Heather Booth

William Winpisinger

1979

MONOPOLY POWER CO.

NO super-profits for ENERGY

UP the PROFITS

Citizen Labor ENERGY Coalition says NO to ENERGY super-profits

1981

I'm happy to announce that I will be co-chair of the new DSA with Michael Harrington.

Barbara Ehrenreich

MLK march, 20th anniversary, 1983...

WE STILL HAVE A DREAM

DSA

The Socialist of the region, Jamaica's prime minister, Michael Manley.

THE SOCIALIST INTERNA

2017 The change came almost too late, Labor's conservatives had let the movement go down the drain. But unions will fight on!

fight for DEMOCRATIC SOCIALISM

DSA

DEMOCRATIC SOCIALISTS OF AMERICA

Bernie Sanders

I believe in a society where all people do well, not just a handful of billionaires!

Portland rally, march, 2016

...that if he or she does their school work--

A FUTURE TO BELIEVE IN

BERNIE

A FUTURE TO BELIEVE IN

A FUTURE TO BELIEVE IN

HOP

A FUTURE TO BELIEVE IN

I think there may be some symbolism here. I know it doesn't look like it, but that little bird is actually a dove asking us for world peace!

NO MORE WARS!

FUTURE TO BELIEVE IN

BERNIE

A FUTURE TO BELIEVE IN

Bernie is a long-distance runner with integrity in the struggle for justice over 50 years.

Cornel West

FURTHER READING

Buhle, Mari Jo, Paul Buhle, and Dan Georgakas, eds. *Encyclopedia of the American Left*. 2nd edition. New York: Oxford University Press, 1998.

Constantine, J. Robert, ed. *Letters of Eugene V. Debs*. Vols. I–III. Urbana: University of Illinois, 1990.

Freeberg, Ernest. *Democracy's Prisoner: Eugene V. Debs, The Great War and the Right to Dissent*. Cambridge, MA: Harvard University Press, 2008.

Ginger, Ray. *The Bending Cross: A Biography of Eugene Victor Debs*. New Brunswick, NJ: Rutgers University Press, 1949.

Gorman, Robert A. *Michael Harrington: Speaking American*. New York: Routledge, 1995.

Harrington, Michael. *Fragments of the Century*. New York: Saturday Review Press, 1972.

Harrington, Michael. *The Long-Distance Runner: An Autobiography*. New York: Henry Holt, 1988.

Harrington, Michael. *Socialism*. New York: Bantam, 1971.

Isserman, Maurice. *The Other American: The Life of Michael Harrington*. New York: Public Affairs, 2000.

Kazin, Michael. *War Against War: The American Fight for Peace, 1914–1918.* New York: Knopf, 2017.

Le Prade, Ruth, ed. *Debs and the Poets.* Pasadena: Upton Sinclair, 1920.

Salvatore, Nick. *Eugene V. Debs, Citizen and Socialist.* Urbana: University of Illinois Press, 2nd edition, 2007.

Sanders, Bernie, with Huck Gutman. *Outsider in the White House,* revised edition. New York: Verso, 2015.

Swanberg, W. A. *Norman Thomas: The Last Idealist.* New York: Charles Scribner's Sons, 1976.

Thomas, Norman. *A Socialist's Faith.* New York: W.W. Norton, 1951.

Graphic Novels (nonfiction)

Buhle, Paul, ed. *A People's History of American Empire.* New York: Metropolitan Books, 2008.

Buhle, Paul, and David Berger, eds. *Bohemians.* New York: Verso, 2014.

Buhle, Paul, and Nicole Schulman, eds. *WOBBLIES!* New York: Verso, 2005.

Jones, Sabrina. *Our Lady of Birth Control: A Cartoonist's Encounter with Margaret Sanger.* New York: Soft Skull Press, 2016.

Rudahl, Sharon. *Dangerous Woman: The Graphic Biography of Emma Goldman.* New York: New Press, 2007.

ACKNOWLEDGMENTS

Verso's Andrew Hsiao eagerly supported this project and, as usual, more than deserves the author's deep gratitude, as does our second editor on the project, Jessie Kindig. As noted in the text, Dave Nance scripted Chapter 4, but also worked with the two editors throughout. We also thank Dolores M. Emspak for her assistance with French translations.

Many thanks are due to our friends at the Democratic Socialists of America (DSA). The "sustaining contributors" noted on the final page gave $500 or more, making the project possible. The moral support of DSA and a sister organization, the Eugene V. Debs Foundation of Terre Haute, Indiana, location of the Debs Homestead, have been all the more vital because of a surge in socialist activity and organization, the largest such in generations.

A very special thanks to Maxine Phillips for her help, encouragement, and comradeship all the way through. Without that help, this book would never have appeared.

LIST OF SUSTAINING CONTRIBUTORS

The Democratic Socialists of America Fund endeavors to demonstrate how an awareness of social democratic and democratic socialist values and policies would strengthen the quality of policy debates in the United States. The Fund also works to introduce young activists to the history and traditions of democratic socialism.

Verso Books and the Fund appreciate all the many contributors who made this volume possible, in particular:

Jules Bernstein and Linda Lipsett
Shannon Hammock
Michael Kazin
Marshall Mayer and Bonnie Lambert
Scott Molloy

Thanks, also, to the many supporters who made contributions in smaller amounts.

The DSA Fund is a 502 (c)(3) fund devoted to education and outreach about democratic socialism.